Keep this pocket-sized Frith
you are travelling around rur

Whether you are in your
enjoy an evocative journey back in time. Compare
the Sussex countryside of old with what you can
see today—see how villages have expanded and
developed, how cottages have been altered or
demolished and shops turned into private houses;
look at fine details such as lamp-posts, shop fascias
and trade signs; and see the many alterations to rural
Sussex that have taken place unnoticed during our
lives, some of which we may have taken for granted.

At the turn of a page you will gain fascinating
insights into the unique history of Sussex.

FRANCIS FRITH'S
pocket ALBUM

VILLAGES OF SUSSEX

A POCKET ALBUM

Adapted from an original book by
ANTHONY BRYAN

FRITH
BOOK Co

First published in the United Kingdom in 2003 by
Frith Book Company Ltd

Reprinted 2003

ISBN 1-85937-720-3

British Library Cataloguing in Publication Data

Villages of Sussex—A Pocket Album
Adapted from an original book by Anthony Bryan

Frith Book Company Ltd
Frith's Barn, Teffont,
Salisbury, Wiltshire SP3 5QP
Tel: +44 (0) 1722 716 376
 Email: info@francisfrith.co.uk
www.francisfrith.co.uk

Printed and bound in Great Britain by MPG, Bodmin

Front Cover: Billingshurst Church Causeway 1912 / 64881

Frontispiece: Charlwood, High Road 1904 52387

*The hand-colouring is for illustrative purposes only, and is not intended to be
historically accurate.*

CONTENTS

FRANCIS FRITH
VICTORIAN PIONEER

Francis Frith, founder of the world-famous photographic archive, was a complex and multi-talented man. A devout Quaker and a highly successful Victorian businessman, he was philosophic by nature and pioneering in outlook. By 1855 he had already established a wholesale grocery business in Liverpool, and sold it for the astonishing sum of £200,000, which is the equivalent today of over £15,000,000. Now in his thirties, and captivated by the new science of photography, Frith set out on a series of pioneering journeys up the Nile and to the Near East.

INTRIGUE AND EXPLORATION

He was the first photographer to venture beyond the sixth cataract of the Nile. Africa was still the mysterious 'Dark Continent', and Stanley and Livingstone's historic meeting was a decade into the future. The conditions for picture taking confound belief. He laboured for hours in his wicker dark-room in the sweltering heat of the desert, while the volatile chemicals fizzed dangerously in their trays. Back in London he exhibited his photographs and was 'rapturously cheered' by members of the Royal Society. His reputation as a photographer was made overnight.

VENTURE OF A LIFE-TIME

By the 1870s the railways had threaded their way across the country, and Bank Holidays and half-day Saturdays had been made obligatory by Act of Parliament. All of a sudden the working man and his family were able to enjoy days out, take holidays, and see a little more of the world.

With typical business acumen, Francis Frith foresaw that these new tourists would enjoy having souvenirs to commemorate their days out. For the next thirty years he travelled the country by train and by pony and trap, producing fine photographs of seaside resorts and beauty spots that were keenly bought by millions of Victorians. These prints were painstakingly pasted into family albums and pored over during the dark nights of winter, rekindling precious memories of summer excursions. Frith's studio was soon supplying retail shops all over the country, and by 1890 F Frith & Co had become the greatest specialist photographic publishing company in the world, with over 2,000 sales outlets, and pioneered the picture postcard.

FRANCIS FRITH'S LEGACY

Francis Frith had died in 1898 at his villa in Cannes, his great project still growing. The archive he created continued in business for another seventy years. By 1970 it contained over a third of a million pictures showing 7,000 British towns and villages.

Frith's legacy to us today is of immense significance and value, for the magnificent archive of evocative photographs he created provides a unique record of change in the cities, towns and villages throughout Britain over a century and more. Frith and his fellow studio photographers revisited locations many times down the years to update their views, compiling for us an enthralling and colourful pageant of British life and character.

We are fortunate that Frith was dedicated to recording the minutiae of everyday life. For it is this sheer wealth of visual data, the painstaking chronicle of changes in dress, transport, street layouts, buildings, housing, engineering and landscape that captivates us so much today, offering us a powerful link with the past and with the lives of our ancestors.

Computers have now made it possible for Frith's many thousands of images to be accessed almost instantly. The archive offers every one of us an opportunity to examine the places where we and our families have lived and worked down the years. Its images, depicting our shared past are now bringing pleasure and enlightenment to millions around the world a century and more after his death.

SUSSEX
AN INTRODUCTION

Sussex is a county of great landscape variations and contrasts, from smooth green hills down to flat marshland, all within quite small distances. The coastline has huge chalk cliffs leading down to shingle beaches; there are also sandy beaches near river estuaries and in the eastern and western extremities. The type of settlement and buildings vary with the local conditions. The pictures in this book are arranged in four sections, Forest, Weald, Downs and Coast—these sections correspond to the differing topography and underlying geology.

FOREST

THE FOREST ridge is the high ground at the northern border of Sussex; from it the land gradually slopes down southwards towards the Weald. It is an area of smaller villages and panoramic views from hilltops. It is forested with mixed woodland that forms an important timber resource. In the past, the forests fuelled a nationally-important iron industry that pre-dated the smelting of iron by using coal. The fuel used was charcoal: this was made from wood as a renewable resource obtained by coppicing managed woodlands. Iron ore was also mined in the forests. Artificial ponds provided water power.

WEALD

The Weald is a flattish region of heavy land situated between the forest ridge and the scarp edge of the South Downs. It is an agricultural region of arable land with fairly small fields and mixed farming. The famous Sussex oak trees can be seen in the woods, hedgerows and fields; the oak trees produced strong timber for shipbuilding and for the framing of half-timbered houses. Large and ever-expanding villages extend along the main roads. Bricks and tiles are made from local mineral deposits, and are used a lot in local building construction. A ridge of sandstone, the Hastings beds, extends from the centre of the Weald south-eastwards and ends in substantial cliffs on the coast at Hastings, near the Conqueror's Castle. Sandstone was used as a building material.

DOWNS

The South Downs are a range of chalk hills extending from Salisbury Plain across Hampshire to the Sussex border, and then south-eastwards across Sussex to Beachy Head. Here, they terminate in slowly eroding cliff faces. The Downs are smooth in contour and mainly grassed over; they are used for sheep and cattle grazing, and sometimes for cornfields. Walking on the South Downs Way is a popular activity – from it there are panoramic views. Downland villages are often small and hilly, with the settlements following natural land contours. Chalk and flint provides building materials, and also lime for improving the land.

COAST

The English Channel forms the southern boundary of Sussex. The South Downs smoothly slope downwards towards the sea, and these lands contain the larger coastal towns. Ports on the coast have brought trade and invaders, and the fishermen who lived in the coastal villages provided fresh food. The beaches were a vast source of flint pebbles, which were widely used as walling for buildings and land enclosure.

A lot of the smaller villages have now been absorbed into nearby towns. Villages with harbours have been conserved, and retain a lot of their old-world charm, and coastal hamlets survive, some at the top of high cliffs, with great coastal views. Shingle beaches are a feature of the central part of the coastline, while sandy beaches are found near the river estuaries and the flat areas to the eastern and western extremities of the coastline and in the sandstone cliff area near Hastings.

VILLAGE LIFE

Village life was centred on the shop, public house, church, village hall, school, telephone kiosk and bus stop and shelter, and all were bound together by the availability of local employment. Examples of these are seen in the pictures. The postal service is important to village life. Most villages have a Post Office: many are pictured in this book, together with posting boxes and stamp vending machines.

Modes of travel have progressed from the time when local workers walked to their workplace, and when wealthy people used horse-drawn carriages and stagecoaches for local and trunk travel. When the stone-chip roads were smooth enough, the bicycle was useful for local personal travel. Motor transport came along with smoother roads, and enabled more journeys to the towns. Railways provided some villages with reliable travel to anywhere in the country. In recent years, the construction of international railways and airports has made journeys to anywhere in the world quickly accessible from anywhere in Sussex.

FITTLEWORTH, THE VILLAGE 1921 / 70080

Sussex has many large country estates; in private ownership, they were a complete and very self-sufficient entity. Their main business was agricultural and horticultural production, together with pleasure activities. The very large estates had their own timberyards, brickworks and blacksmiths, and they also retained their own building tradesmen. Some villages were created solely to service the needs of a country estate. Many country estates have now been dispersed by being sold in separate lots.

Changes in village life from 1900 to 1950 were greatly accelerated by two world wars. Government control of agriculture in both world wars caused big changes in country life, which were mainly brought about by enforced mechanisation. Agricultural workers who could be spared were called up into the armed services; this caused wartime shortages of male workers, which led to a much greater use of female workers on farms and in rural industries. By the end of both wars, fewer manual workers were needed in agriculture, and draught animals were progressively phased out. Village war memorials are seen in several of our photographs. Also, many country estates did not survive the two wars intact. This was partly owing to shortages of labour and materials. Many large country houses were requisitioned by the government for wartime purposes, and did not return to family domestic use. Labour costs rose after the Second World War, so estate workers were kept to a minimum. Several Sussex country houses were war-damaged, but this was often owing to unfortunate accidents rather than enemy action.

The changes in village life since 1950 happened in a sequence that is still progressing. Personal transport was a catalyst of change - the bicycle, the motor cycle and then the car. The motor car caused the really big change, which was from about 1960 onwards. At first, the car was used as family transport, for shopping and for exploration on trips and holidays. From 1980 onwards, the car became personal transport, so that several members of a family could work, socialise and shop in different places. The increasing use of road transport in villages is recorded in our photographs. The effect of family and personal transport on village life was that the profitability of the local shop was greatly reduced, and so was the viability of rural bus routes. The shops became run-down, and many closed because they could not compete on price and variety of goods with the new supermarkets in the towns. Bus routes were cut back, and smaller vehicles operated a reduced service to fewer destinations.

Very recent changes affecting village life are the mobile telephone and high fuel and car ownership costs. The mobile phone has brought personal communication to all, wherever they may be, so public telephone kiosks are little-used and non-viable. High fuel costs make energy-efficient homes desirable. High transport costs reduce the profitability of commuting, so working from home is attractive. High fuel costs may help village shops to survive as convenience stores, for it is not economic to travel far to a shop by car to collect small orders. We can see many examples of small village shops in the photographs in this book.

The existence of large international airports in the region affects village life considerably, even where aircraft noise is not a problem. Airports employ thousands of shift workers who need personal transport to get to work, so they prefer to live in the countryside. This all brings life, employment and prosperity to an up-to-date village. New developments of large modern family homes in and around villages have brought an influx of new residents, and the conversion of older houses and agricultural buildings into dwellings has become very popular. Village public houses (we can see many pubs pictured in this book) have survived, because many now offer restaurant facilities which suit a modern lifestyle.

Ticehurst is an old Roman habitation near the Kent border. Situated on a hilltop in rolling countryside among hopfields, it has fine views. The Duke of York Inn is on the left-hand side of the square, and the church is nearby.

TICEHURST

THE SQUARE 1925 / 76997

Wadhurst is high up in the forest ridge and was noted for its market and iron industry. Here, a sign outside the old barber's shop offers 'Shaving', while tools and hardware stand outside another shop. A fine sign overhangs the road—it reads 'The Queen's Head Commercial Hotel, C Tulley proprietor'. High Street was devastated in 1956 by an air accident involving a Meteor jet fighter aircraft. Many buildings were destroyed, including The Queens Head Hotel, and have been replaced by modern shop units.

WADHURST

HIGH STREET 1903 / W4501

Frant is 600 feet above sea level and has extensive views. Most of the houses are positioned around the large green where there were once old archery butts. Just off the main through road, H Kemp, Stores and Post Office, is still trading. In the 12th century King John had a hunting lodge in the area. The 15th-century church of St Alban was rebuilt in 1822. Iron smelting and gunfounding brought prosperity to the area in the 16th century. Eridge Old Park is a deer park with a large lake; there is also an observatory tower on Saxonbury Hill on the site of an Iron Age hill-fort. Shernfold Park is a Victorian house of 1853.

FRANT

THE POST OFFICE c1955 / F173002

ERIDGE GREEN

THE NEVILL CREST AND GUN c1950 / E214008

This inn is named after the Earl of Warwick, Richard Nevill. He was known as the Kingmaker and lived in Eridge Castle, the ancestral seat of the Marquis of Abergavenny. The lands of Eridge have been in the hands of the Nevill family in a direct male line from 1450. The scene is much the same today, with business continuing beside the busy main road.

GROOMBRIDGE

THE WALKS, OLD TOWN c1960 / G203053

We are on the upper River Medway north of the Ashdown Forest, near the Kent border. The 13th-century church of St Mary is on a knoll in the centre of the village. The Lychgate, c1520, is a half-timbered cottage by the churchyard with an upper floor extending above. Bolebrooke was a 16th-century brick mansion, once the home of the Dalyngrigge and Sackville families; only fragments survive.

HARTFIELD

THE VILLAGE 1906 / 56691

A small village on the edge of the Ashdown Forest, east of Forest Row. Holy Trinity church was built towards the end of the last century and features a copy of an Italian Pieta by Francesco Francia. Nearby Hollyhill is a large house with a Jacobean façade built in 1885. In the picture, heavy horses wait patiently by the stable while they are prepared for work. On the roofline a builder stands on a scaffolding platform repairing a chimneystack.

COLEMANS HATCH

THE HATCH INN 1927 / 79599

We are on the Eastbourne to London main road. Outside the stables of the Shelley Arms Hotel, a large 18th century coaching inn, produce stalls display items for sale. A car speeds past—the event was recorded on slow film, so the image is blurred. Nearby is Nutley windmill, an open trestle post mill that has been restored to working order and is open to visitors.

NUTLEY

THE HOTEL 1928 / 80744

A large village on the northern edge of the Ashdown Forest, Forest Row was a popular place in the 14th century when the King and his Lords used it as a base for hunting. Brambletye was the first mansion in the area; it was built in 1631 and destroyed by 1680. The ruins are extant. A new Brambletye was built nearby in 1919. The main road leads down past Holy Trinity church, which was built in 1836. The scene is similar today but the road is very busy with motor traffic.

FOREST ROW

THE VILLAGE 1909 / 61439

We are at the eastern edge of the Ashdown Forest. Waiting at the bus stop is a nearly new open-top Leyland double-decker bus with an outside staircase. It is on route 92, Eastbourne to East Grinstead. A small lorry waits outside the Ashdown Garage. Not far away are Chelwood Vachery, a re-created hall-house originally called Trimmer's Pond, and Kidbrooke Park, a much altered and decorated house with gardens laid out by Repton.

CHELWOOD GATE

THE VILLAGE c1930 / C76501

This area was connected with the Sussex iron industry in the 17th century. The forests had deposits of iron ore, and supplies of wood fuel to smelt it; the iron-making families brought much wealth to the parish. The church of St Margaret, with a shingled broach spire, stands above the houses. The neat topiary hedge-work seen on the left is in the garden of the 15th-century Priest's House, which is open to visitors.

WEST HOATHLY

THE VILLAGE c1950 / W64009

This is a small village beside an old Roman route through the Worth
Forest. The Church of All Saints was built in 1843. In our photograph,
the village stores and post office were sheltered from the roadway behind
trimmed hedges. The old Post Office is now a house and the front
gardens have been lost owing to the widening of the very busy road.

CRAWLEY DOWN

THE VILLAGE c1950 / C529001

ARDINGLY

Ardingly is a village overlooking the Ouse valley, north of Haywards Heath. The 14th-century church of St Peter has an impressive tower. Ardingly College, situated nearby, is a notable Public School. Wakehurst Place, built in 1590, is a country estate with substantial ornamental gardens and tree collections. Now in the care of the National Trust, it is run by the Royal Botanical Gardens, Kew.

Copthorne was a new parish, formed in 1881 out of Worth and Crawley Down. The church of St John Evangelist was built in 1877 and is just in Sussex. The picture shows local shops with a proliferation of signs of all types outside; vending machines are attached to the shopfront. An obtrusive clutter of tall poles lines the road, and a modern concrete street lamp does little to enhance the scene. The roadside has been cleared up considerably in recent years. The Prince Albert public house is at the end of the road, hidden by trees.

COPTHORNE

THE VILLAGE c1955 / C422038

Worth village stands in the Forest of Worth, east of Crawley, and was a place of pilgrimage. The fine Anglo-Saxon church of St Nicholas was a principal church in pre-Conquest times. The 18th-century Worth Abbey is on the site of a town house called Paddockhurst. It is now run by the Benedictine Order as a monastery and public school. In the picture we see the Priest's House and the lychgate; both have Horsham stone roofing.

WORTH

THE LYCHGATE AND THE CHURCH c1960 / W146003

This village is noted for its beautiful woods, a railway tunnel under the Balcombe Forest and a brick viaduct over the Ouse valley. The church of St Mary was built in 1847. Balcombe House, once called Parsonage House, is a large Tudor-style house of 1856. The 13th-century White House was run by the White Friars as a hostelry for Canterbury pilgrims. In this picture are three shops, including G G Newing Stores, later C G Smith, and Balcombe Stores, the grocer. The young girl pedestrian has little traffic to worry about.

BALCOMBE

THE VILLAGE c1955 / B503006

The village was named after the bridges crossing the River Mole. The picture shows a well-stocked corner shop dealing in general and fancy drapery, and acting also as a Postal Telegraph office. Window displays include net curtaining, boots and shoes and hats. The shopfront and street corner have gas lamps, and the small front gardens have wood fencing. A boy waits near the shop doorway, watching the Frith photographer.

THREE BRIDGES

THE POST OFFICE 1906 / 55383

HORLEY

STATION ROAD 1905 / 53298

Horley is on the old main London to Brighton road before it was diverted around the area of new Gatwick airport. Single and two-horse traps wait by the roadside. Corn and coal merchants sell proprietary animal feeds. We can also see London House, a draper's, Branch's shop, a dairy and a game and poultry shop. A line of very tall telegraph poles are topped with pointed finials. Sunblinds are extended on the side of the street facing the sun.

Lowfield Heath is near the old London to Brighton main road. The White Lion Inn, left, also serves teas. The Stores, run by J F Mitchell, has the door open awaiting customers. In the background is St Michael's church. Built in 1867, it has a square tower and a pyramidal spire. The whole area is now very close to the greatly expanded and very busy Gatwick Airport, which was built in the 1960s partly on the site of the old Gatwick racecourse.

LOWFIELD HEATH

THE CHURCH AND THE VILLAGE 1905 / 53328

A village on the eastern edge of the St Leonards Forest at a high point on the London to Brighton trunk road. The Red Lion, c1550, is an old coaching inn. Nymans Gardens has an ornate dovecote and is in the care of the National Trust and open to visitors. Handcross Park house is now a school. The buildings in the photograph are little changed today. The village was by-passed in 1959.

HANDCROSS

HIGH STREET c1950 / H311003

A hilltop village on the southern edge of the Worth Forest with distant views of both the North and South Downs. St Leonard's church was built in 1895. The Crown is a 16th-century coaching inn and has a turnspit and crane in a fireplace. The corner shop is located on a crossroads at the highest point in the village. A large chapel is nearby. The scene today is very similar.

TURNERS HILL

THE CORNER SHOP AND THE CHAPEL c1960 / T248044

CHARLWOOD

THE ARCHWAY 1906 / 54173

A small village at the western edge of St Leonards Forest, on the main road and railway line between Horsham and Crawley. Local legends say that dragons and serpents inhabited the forest. Charcoal-making was a forest industry until the 1960s, and was carried out on sites within the forest. There were two brick works in the village. A road of brick cottages is seen next to the Wesleyan church. The scene has now altered: the left-hand side of the road has been developed with houses and bungalows, and the church is now converted to a house.

FAYGATE

THE VILLAGE 1929 / 82454

A small village on minor roads near to the Surrey border. The church of St Mary Magdalene has two historic 14th-century brasses. In the 12th century, a small Benedictine convent known as Rusper Priory was founded by a small number of nuns. The last remnants of the convent were demolished in 1781. The picture shows Friday Street, with the historic Plough Inn on the left, obscured from view by a large tree. The village store is on the right halfway down the road. The scene is similar today.

RUSPER

THE VILLAGE 1909 / 61383

We are just north-west of Horsham. The church of St Margaret's has a neatly clipped yew tunnel at the churchyard entrance. Inside is an elaborate monument to the memory of John Caryll, an ironmaster. Warnham watermill is on the site of an iron furnace; it has been nicely restored to workable order. The picture shows a neatly sculptured hedge topped with fine topiary peacocks. Stone flag pavements line the road. Brickmaking is an important local industry: a hundred million bricks were made a year in the 1970s. The topiary yew hedge is now grown out; otherwise the scene is still similar.

WARNHAM

TOPIARY WORK 1928 / 80850

A small village with a common on the Portsmouth to Guildford main road near the Hampshire border. Chalk quarrying is carried out on the hills here. We are right on the border here—part of the inn is in Hampshire. The name of the inn comes from two stagecoaches, 'The Fly' and 'The Bull', which plied the road. Cars of the early motor age travel along the road, or wait at the side. Large telegraph poles line the road.

RAKE

THE FLYING BULL 1934 / 86051

An estate village of Hollycombe, a Tudor-style house of c1900. Chapel Common has a quaint 16th-century chapel in a wood, with a new church of St Luke built nearby in 1878. In the picture an old farmhouse stands next to farm buildings; the two semi-detached stone cottages alongside probably housed farm workers.

MILLAND

COTTAGES 1901 / 46598

41

We are on the Petworth to Guildford main road. The church of St John Baptist was rebuilt in 1877; it has a strange-looking font dated 1662. The Half Moon is a 16th-century inn. The Swan Inn can be seen down the road beyond the horse-drawn vehicles that are waiting for the Frith photographer.

NORTHCHAPEL

THE VILLAGE 1902 / 48369

The village was a Roman settlement with a tile works. It later became a centre for the iron industry with a furnace, a forge and a cannon foundry. The church of St Margaret has Norman walling and windows. Hawksfold was the home of Anthony Salvin, an eminent architect. The Verdley Place Estate of 1870 is now occupied by an agricultural chemical manufacturer. Blackdown is a great sandstone hill 918 feet high, and Blackdown House is a Tudor-style manor house of 1640.

FERNHURST

VANN ROAD 1908 / 59675

KINGSLEY GREEN, HINDHEAD

FROM THE TOLL HOUSE 1910 / 63047

The Sussex Turnpike Trust was set up in 1749 to maintain the road from Hindhead Heath to Chichester with a tollgate at Kingsley Marsh (now Green). Regular users of the roads became skilled at dodging toll collection points. The picture could easily be mistaken for a more modern scene. There is nothing visible that gives clues to the real date.

Bodiam is located on the River Rother and was once a port that shipped iron ingots and cannon, which were made in the area. Bodiam Castle was constructed in 1388, the last castle to be built in England for coastal defence. In the picture we can see the 14th-century Castle Inn on the right and Bodiam Stores on the left. The scene is similar today, but the shop is now a tearoom.

BODIAM

THE VILLAGE C1955 / B128015

ROBERTSBRIDGE

HIGH STREET c1955 / R332034

BURWASH

THE VILLAGE 1889 / B291501

Flimwell is centred on a crossroads near the Kent border. Its church, St Augustine's, was built in 1873. Seacox is a French chateau- style house built in 1871 for the Goschen family, who were great benefactors of the village; they built a number of cottages for estate staff. Sir Edward Goschen was British Ambassador in Berlin in 1914 when the war began. Seacox Park has a magnificent collection of trees and shrubs.

FLIMWELL

THE VILLAGE 1903 / 49363

The 'Cuckoo Trail' for cyclists, walkers and the disabled connects Horam to Heathfield and Polegate via the route of an old railway. Old industries in the area were iron ore mining and brickmaking, which is expected to be revived soon. Horeham Manor is noted for making Merrydown vintage cider. The village sign is in the left foreground of the picture. Passengers board the route 91 Southdown bus, en route from Uckfield to Eastbourne.

HORAM

THE POST OFFICE c1955 / H329009

Windmill Hill is near Herstmonceux. It is a post-type windmill where the body is turned to the wind by means of a long tail-pole. The front and sides of the mill body and the roundhouse roof are clad in sheet iron. It is the tallest windmill of this type in Sussex. Built in 1814, it ceased working in 1893, when the sails were taken off. There was a bakery by the mill house. The mill is now being restored by its owner. Iron electricity poles line the road; they are of a type only seen in this part of Sussex.

WINDMILL HILL

C1965 / W448005

The village is named after five ash trees on the green. Twits Gill was once the home of Sir Austen Chamberlain, who was Chancellor of the Exchequer in 1903 and Foreign Secretary in the 1920s. He assembled a vast collection of rock plants from all over the world. At the time of the picture, the Five Ashes public house was offering customers ales from Tamplins, Brighton Brewery.

FIVE ASHES

THE FIVE ASHES INN c1960 / F172002

We are in the Cuckmere Valley, with fine views of the scarp side of the Downs. The Dicker, behind the brick wall and trees beyond the pub, is a rather odd-looking mansion, built by Horatio William Bottomley, a politician and journalist. The building is now occupied by St Bede's School. Dicker Pottery made bricks, tiles and pottery. Not far away is Michelham Priory, founded in 1229 for 13 Augustinian Canons. The inn in the photograph is offering Tamplins Brighton Ales.

UPPER DICKER

THE PLOUGH INN c1950 / U50004

BLACKBOYS

THE POST OFFICE c1960 / B566034

Blackboys is a small iron industry village. Its name is believed to have come from the appearance of charcoal workers as they emerged from working in the woods. The village also had a well-known post-type windmill, which was sited by the main road. The 14th-century Blackboys Inn has been recently restored after fire damage.

One of many millponds used by the Sussex iron industry. The ponds stored water to drive waterwheels for powering furnace blowers, forging hammers for working wrought iron, and for driving lathes for boring cannon. Boringwheel Mill is nearby; it finished work as a corn mill site. Just visible on the hilltop is the spire of the church of St Bartholomew. The Chequers is an old coaching inn built in 1734.

MARESFIELD

THE MILL POND 1902 / 48216

HALLAND

We are on the Eastbourne main road, south of Uckfield. Halland Park Farm is the remains of the mansion built in 1595 to replace Laughton Place as the principal house of the Pelham family. The Blacksmith's Arms is made out of extended and altered buildings, with a house at the core. The village store has been added to the front and side of what was once a large house.

Simon de Montfort's army lay here the night before the Battle of Lewes in 1264. The area was made notorious by the 'Piltdown Man' fake archaeological discoveries in the 1910s. The nearby Sheffield Park estate built the modern mock half-timbered houses seen at the far end of the street. Sheffield Park Gardens were magnificently landscaped by Capability Brown and are open to visitors. They also contain the National Pinetum collection of pine trees. The southern terminus station of the Bluebell Railway to East Grinstead is nearby.

FLETCHING

THE STREET c1950 / F138005

Newick is situated halfway between two great Christian centres of worship—Canterbury and Winchester—so the village was used as a resting-place for pilgrims. A range of different building styles is seen in the picture, including the Bull Inn, whose sign stands on the green in front.

NEWICK

THE GREEN c1955 / N90009

A scattered village on a hilltop in the centre of Sussex. Friendly societies began here at the Five Bells Inn in 1782. The Heritage is a specialised health care institution for disabled children with buildings in several locations around the area. High Common was famous for potteries, and bricks are still made in the area. North Common has a white smock windmill reckoned to be the exact centre of Sussex.

CHAILEY

THE VILLAGE GREEN c1965 / C437004

There are connections with the Sussex iron industry, for an ironmaster once lived here. The 17th-century house Birch Grove was the home of Harold Macmillan, the former Prime Minister. Ludwell Grange, built in 1540, is a fine half-timbered house. The Norman church of St Giles is at the north end of the village. Along a footpath nearby is a well-restored watermill with a wooden overshot waterwheel. The railway station is on the Bluebell Line to East Grinstead. The village stores has been made by adapting a house.

HORSTED KEYNES

THE GREEN c1965 / H359017

The church of St John the Baptist is mainly 13th-century and has a wood-shingled broach spire. The village has many historic houses. The Bower House is a timber-framed hall house with a kingpost roof. The Tiger public house was once Church House—behind the brick façade it has a king post roof and a 15th-century hall. The half-timbered Thatched Cottage was built c1390 by the Chaloner family, who were French immigrant broadloom blanket weavers. Humphrey's Bakery, High Street, has been dated 1332

LINDFIELD

THE BOWER HOUSE AND THE CHURCH c1955 / L221060

Keymer is at the foot of the Downs near Hassocks. The Norman church of St Cosmos and St Damian was re-built in 1866. Ockley Manor is an 18th-century brick house, with a dovecote. Oldland post windmill is being slowly restored to a good state of repair. On the left of the picture is the signboard of the Greyhound, a Watneys house. It has a fireplace dated 1595.

KEYMER

KEYMER ROAD c1960 / K127028

WHITEMANS GREEN

THE VILLAGE c1965 / W452011

*A small village to the north of Cuckfield, Whiteman's
Green was once on several bus routes—a single-decker
bus is just visible at the bottom of the hill. A village sign
is on grass verge. It is nice to see a village scene with no
visible overhead wires and poles.*

Bolney is a quiet village, located just off the main London to Brighton trunk road. The 13th-century church of St Mary Magdalene has a massive 16th-century tower with rounded pinnacles, which houses the peal of eight bells. The public house is appropriately named the Eight Bells. A timber-framed Tudor Tea House is located on the main road. A new vineyard was planted in the village in 1973.

BOLNEY

THE POST OFFICE 1957 / B507050

Henfield is a main road village midway between Horsham and Brighton. St Peter's 13th-century church was rebuilt in 1870. Brickmaking was quite a large local industry. A common on the Brighton Road has a fine cricket pitch and reed beds. There are two old coaching inns in the High Street: the 14th-century George and the White Hart. In the picture an old-style touring caravan hitched up to its towing car waits at the roadside.

HENFIELD

GOLDEN SQUARE c1955 / H313002

PARTRIDGE GREEN

THE MILL c1950 / P60300

The village was created at the turn of the century to house construction workers for the very large brick-built Christ's Hospital school nearby. The famous poet Shelley was born at nearby Field Place. Broadbridge Mill is an ancient mill site by the River Arun. It was a prosperous business powered by two waterwheels that drove six pairs of millstones. The village is now cut off by the new Horsham by-pass that takes much traffic out of the village. The scene in the picture is still recognisable.

BROADBRIDGE HEATH

THE PORTSMOUTH AND GUILDFORD ROADS 1924 / 75469

Good's Stores, bakery, Post Office and café was fire-damaged in the 1970s. The site has now been redeveloped for housing. The Blue Idol is a Quaker Friends Meeting House and guesthouse which was converted for William Penn in 1691. The Selsey Arms Inn is half-timbered with a more recent façade. It has a dog-wheel that once drove a meat roasting spit in an inglenook fireplace. Nearby is a memorial to a World War Two fighter airfield, which was used by the American Air Force.

COOLHAM

THE POST OFFICE AND STORES c1950 / C424006

A scattered hillside village on a minor road in a wooded area near the Surrey border. Mushroom growing, brick making and fullers earth extraction were local industries. The King's Head was built in 1733; not originally a public house, it had a cellar to store stalls for an annual fair held nearby. The Rising Sun on top of the pub sign was a trademark of Brickwoods (Portsmouth) brewery. The scene is similar today.

RUDGWICK

THE KING'S HEAD c1965 / R305052

BILLINGSHURST

CHURCH CAUSEWAY 1912 / 64881

Billingshurst is a Roman settlement on Stane Street. St Mary's church, built on a mound with access to the churchyard via a causeway, is shown here, and has Roman bricks in the walls. The scene is similar today, but the road is metalled and very busy with motor traffic. The shop has since been converted to a private house.

A small village, built to house Parham Estate employees, Cootham is situated near to the foot of the downs. Nearby Parham Park has a fine Elizabethan mansion that is open to visitors during the summer months. The picture shows the common with the village in the background. The young girls are dressed up and stand still for the photographer.

COOTHAM

THE VILLAGE 1894 / 34411

PULBOROUGH

ST MARY'S CHURCH 1939 / 88914

A Roman settlement on Stane Street and the navigable River Arun. The village encompasses riverside and hillside, and has a main line railway station. The 15th-century church is on the hillside. The photograph shows the view from the side of Stane Street, which is now very busy. The scene now is little changed, although the almshouses have been converted into one house.

WISBOROUGH GREEN

THE CHURCH AND THE VILLAGE 1896 / 38179

This is a fine view of a pastoral hillside. The church of St Peter ad Vincula has a shingled broach spire. We can see a splendid smock windmill in full working order in the left distance. It was built about 1820, ceased work 1910, and was demolished in 1915. The two-storey sandstone base is now part of a house.

Fittleworth is a picturesque village of fine old houses, commons and fir woods. The local people call this 'Hallelujah Corner' because it is a sharp bend on a narrow and busy main road, near the church of St Mary. The house on the right of the picture has a chimneystack that is heavily overgrown by creeper, in later years removed.

FITTLEWORTH
THE VILLAGE 1908 / 60183

Located in a remote region north of Petworth, the village was originally formed in a clearing in the woods. The local wealden clay district is remarkable for large oak trees. In the iron industry era there were smelting furnaces and forges here; Sussex marble was also dug in the area. Holy Trinity church is shown here, with turret, clock and spire and a Horsham stone roof. Outside the village store an enamelled metal sign advertises Bluebell Metal Polish. The Sun Inn is on the right behind bushes. The scene is now little changed, although the shop has gone.

PLAISTOW

THE VILLAGE c1955 / P301012

GRAFFHAM

THE VILLAGE c1955 / G195013

LOXWOOD

THE STORES c1955 / L304001

Loxwood is on the route of the partly-restored Wey and Arun canal near the Surrey border— 'London's lost route to the sea'. The shop on the left has old enamelled metal cigarette advertising signs fixed to the wall. There is a larger shop across road. A woman waits patiently against the fence by the pond; she has just come from the swimming pool area.

EASEBOURNE

THE VILLAGE 1906 / 55444

This village near Midhurst was built mainly to house employees of the Cowdray Estate, famed for the landscaped park and polo playing. There are cart tracks in the loose, unsealed road surface. Children wait at the roadside, perhaps for transport to school. Easebourne was built mainly to house employees of the Cowdray Estate,

We are in a valley of the Downs near Beachy Head. Here we see a workplace with an open-air view; the craftsmen are taking a breather. Apparatus for wheelwrighting is nearby, and there is an iron cone for forging circular iron rings and a flat circular area for laying out wheels. The yoke hung on the front wall was used for draught animals, most probably oxen. A tall white flagpole stands in the garden.

EASTDEAN

THE OLD FORGE 1921 / 71405

We are on the slope of the Downs between Eastbourne and Polegate. A nearby vantage point at Combe hill is 638 feet high. The village church of St Mary's is an Early English building with an ancient chest and coffin. Opposite the church is the Hoo, a large rambling house built in 1902. The Post Office proprietor was R F Brierley; alongside is the entrance to the builders' and decorators' yard, F J French & Sons.

WILLINGDON

THE POST OFFICE c1950 / W446007

A Saxon settlement beside the River Cuckmere, Alfriston was a centre for smuggling. We can see old shops in the photograph— S Selvey, the grocer, and Wood, the butcher. The ancient market cross has been knocked down by vehicles and restored several times. The scene is similar today, and well conserved, but all the shops are now engaged in tourist-related trading.

ALFRISTON

MARKET SQUARE c1955 / A33017

LITLINGTON

This leafy flint village is situated in the Cuckmere valley near Alfriston. Nearby is one of the smallest Neolithic long barrows in Sussex. In the picture the Stores has a sign offering 'Morning coffee and light refreshments, Teas'. There is still a very good tea garden here.

Sedlescombe is a hillside village near Battle, with a large green. A local mill made the best gunpowder in Europe. An iron pot containing a large number of coins of Edward the Confessor was found in 1876. They were thought to have belonged to King Harold, and hidden during the Battle of Hastings. The pump house, dated 1900, was a centre of village life before piped mains water supplies. An iron cage protects the ornate lead pump head.

SEDLESCOMBE

THE VILLAGE PUMP c1955 / S494009

This area was connected with the iron industry. The church has a Tudor doorway and a Norman piscina on a carved pillar. Thomas Turner, who lived in the village in the mid-18th century, left an important diary spanning eleven years of his life. The Pelham family were influential local landowners, and their emblem was the Pelham Buckle; cast iron milestones in the area have the Pelham Buckle carved on them. The village is noted for trug manufacture at a local steamed wood works.

EAST HOATHLY

SOUTH STREET c1950 / E177006

We are on the Downs, just north of Seaford. The church of St Peter has a fine Norman fonty. Admiral Walker, who fought with Nelson, is buried here. In 1794 a very large barracks was built just north of the village; it was used to house militia during the Napoleonic Wars. After the First World War, the barracks were closed and demolished. The village is now a part of Seaford; it is surrounded by recent housing estates, although the scene is still recognisable.

EAST BLATCHINGTON

THE VILLAGE 1891 / 28388

Glynde is most famous for its internationaly renowned opera house built in the grounds of Glyndbourne. In this view of the village the old building on the left is timber-framed with a false façade. It has been rendered, tile-hung and weather-boarded, and substantial porches have been added. Horizontally sliding lights are fitted in some of the windows. On the right-hand side of the winding village street stand flint-walled houses with brick dressings.

GLYNDE

THE SQUARE c1955 / G202010

A range of 16th-century houses and cottages descends the hill towards a central crossroads, notably Old Forge, Bowries and Ricksteddle. St Margaret's church has a 13th-century oak chest and 14th-century glass. The village is now noted as an art and craft centre. Ditchling Beacon is a famous vantagepoint 813 feet up on the Downs with panoramic views. There are dewponds alongside the road by the Beacon.

DITCHLING

HIGH STREET c1960 / D158097

We are on the Downs between Brighton and Lewes. Near the rebuilt church there is a thatched barn and an early dewpond. Dewponds were depressions in the chalk ground, lined with puddled clay; they were used to collect rainfall for watering farm livestock. The village is now cut in two by a very busy dual carriageway, and is the location of the University of Sussex campus. The scene is similar today, but most properties are now used by the university.

FALMER

THE VILLAGE c1955 / F170001

Bramber is located at the foot of a Norman castle guarding the tidal River Adur. The village was a popular coach trip destination from the coastal resorts; now visitors travel in their cars. It is now largely residential with pubs and restaurants. Lavender Cottage dates back to the 15th century. In those days the sea came much closer, and it used to be a fisherman's home. It is reputed to have a tunnel between the grounds and a nearby castle; it was used by an amorous couple to visit each other.

BRAMBER

THE VILLAGE STREET c1950 / B179007

WASHINGTON

THE POST OFFICE c1960 / W359019

Washington is on the main London to Worthing Road at the foot of the Downs. There are fine views of Chanctonbury Ring, a ring of beech trees planted on the site of an Iron Age hill fort 800 feet up on the top of the Downs. In the picture the Post Office has signs advertising tobacco and cigarettes fixed to the shop front, with an Esso paraffin sign further along. The large door of the outbuilding has a cat hole.

Findon is on the top of the Downs, just north of Worthing, and was noted for an annual sheep fair. Now horse breeding and training is an important local activity. Findon Place is a manor house built in the 13th century and extended around the year 1740, with extensive stables added in 1800. Cissbury Ring is an Iron Age fort, with flint mines, 602 feet up on the Downs to the east. The Post Office has a pillar-box with a sign on top with an arrow pointing to the entrance a few feet away.

FINDON

POST OFFICE CORNER c1960 / F131091

We are in a marshy area—Amberley Wild Brooks, beside the tidal and navigable River Arun. The castle was a fortified manor of the Bishops of Chichester; it was crenellated c1377 to defend the coastal area and the river estuary. The varying height of the old houses built of flint and stone with thatch and tile, contrasts with the varying width of the roadway. It is now a village where artists like to work.

AMBERLEY

THE VILLAGE c1960 / A44008

This is Old Durrington windmill, photographed at a time when the site was used as a tea garden. Only two sails were on the mill at this time. The white tailpole was used to turn the body of the mill so that the sails pointed into the wind. It was built about 1720, and ceased work in 1897. The mill is now fully restored and opens to visitors on Sunday afternoons during the summer months.

HIGH SALVINGTON

THE MILL c1955 / H315001

We are on the navigable and tidal River Arun. The church of St John the Evangelist has a shingled broach spire; flint and stone are used for walling and buildings. A ferry with landing steps connected with a foot-path to Amberley on the opposite bank. Novelist and poet John Galsworthy lived in Bury House from 1926 until 1933. The area is now known as Bury Wharf, and the converted farm buildings are used for residential purposes.

BURY

THE CHURCH FROM THE RIVER 1898 / 42556

A secluded village in the middle of the Downs near the Hampshire border, south of Harting. There is a fine Neolithic long barrow on Telegraph Hill, which is 534 feet high. The Norman church of St Mary was rebuilt in 1849, with a timber bell turret and a shingled spire. THis photograph shows the old coaching inn on the Emsworth to Harting road, which sold Henty and Constable's ales at the time of the photograph. The inn is still trading. The scene today is little changed.

COMPTON

THE COACH AND HORSES c1950 / C421018

A random collection of cottages around a pair of lanes forms an oval. The thatch-roofed house has a well-clipped hedge and a Chilean pine—or monkey-puzzle tree—grows in a garden further down the hill. The roadway is of stone; motor transport has not yet arrived. The scene is still recognisable.

EAST HARTING

THE VILLAGE 1906 / 54414

SOUTH HARTING

HIGH STREET c1955 / S820005

We are in the main part of the Hartings, nestling in the northern slopes of the Downs, on the pilgrims' route to Chichester. A brick extension to the front of the terrace of older houses contains the shop; small cigarette advertising signs are fixed to the shopfront. The White Hart Inn is next door with an old type of telephone box outside. At the road junction we see the Ship Inn.

This village is justt below the Downs on the main road between Midhurst and Chichester. The church has a 14th-century tower, and a mural painting in the nave dated 1220. The rebuilt Manor House is nearby. The locality is excellent for rambling over the Downs. In this superb picture three children are dressed up in their best clothes and keep still for the photographer.

COCKING

THE CHURCH 1906 / 54384

105

Woodstock House is a country house hotel nestling in the Downs below the heights of Charlton Forest. We are near Goodwood racecourse, hence the racing scene on the hotel restaurant signboard. The buildings have flint walls and thatched, tiled and slate roofing. The rendered and painted façade in the central building probably conceals an older building. Nearby are Goodwood House and Park, built in 1660 and greatly extended in 1760. It is The Duke of Richmond's estate, and has fine art collections.

CHARLTON

WOODSTOCK HOUSE C1955 / C418002

We are on the southern slope of the Downs, north of Chichester. Boxgrove Priory, of the Benedictine Order, was founded in 1105. At its dissolution in 1537, the priory church became the parish church dedicated to St Mary and St Blaise. The picture shows the road past the school with the Priory on the right. The scene today is little changed.

BOXGROVE

THE VILLAGE c1960 / B167027

Houghton is a hamlet with a long stone bridge across the tidal River Arun. The inn is a 13th-century timber-framed brick and flint building. King Charles II is said to have taken refreshments here in 1651 while fleeing from the Battle of Worcester. A Watney's Red Barrel illuminated sign (a much-advertised keg beer of the time) hangs below the main sign.

HOUGHTON

THE GEORGE AND DRAGON c1960 / H515048

Duncton sits at the foot of the Downs, with fine views nearby. Holy Trinity Church was built in 1866 in the Decorated style, on the site of a medieval church. It has the oldest dated bell in Sussex, 1369, which is of Dutch origin. A young girl waits patiently in the field for photographer to finish.

DUNCTON

THE CHURCH 1912 / 64896

WESTHAM

THE VILLAGE c1965 / W373009

This village is in the Ouse valley just north of the town of Newhaven. St John's church is on high ground overlooking the tidal river. It has a Norman flint-built round tower, and a fine shingled octagonal spire. Pottery was a local industry; a conical kiln has been rebuilt and conserved. The sailing cruiser is moored in a mud berth, and local people look on curiously. The village was notorious for smuggling. The scene is more wooded now.

PIDDINGHOE

THE VILLAGE c1955 / P343003

We are very near to Worthing, where the downland has been inhabited ever since pre-historic times. The picture shows Sompting General Supply Stores with a sign fixed to the shopfront advertising Players Weights cigarettes, a popular budget brand. On the opposite side of the road, Smugglers has signs offering teas and homemade cakes—no fast food yet.

SOMPTING

WEST STREET c1955 / S148004

Ferring is a residential village near the sea. The Norman church keeps the registers of Kingston, a village long lost due to coastal erosion. Highdown Hill, 269 feet high, was a Roman dwelling place and Saxon burial ground. In the picture we can see a bus stop sign on a concrete post, for Southdown route 106 only, Worthing to South Ferring. Marsh's stores and Ferring Motors' garage are on the opposite side of the road.

FERRING

THE VILLAGE c1955 / F130051

Broadwater is the old parish on which Worthing was built; its church is the mother church of the town. It was an old market under the Camois family, and is now a district of Worthing. In the picture we see large houses with garden walls of flint. Children wait on the pavement and road edge to be included in the Frith photograph. Women in long skirts walk along, or wait on the opposite pavement. Horse-drawn vehicles travel along the road, which has a fairly smooth surface and proper pavements.

BROADWATER

THE VILLAGE 1906 / 56721

A rapidly expanding village, just inland from the coastline. The great house was New Place; it has now been converted into cottages. It was the home of the Palmer family in the time of Henry VIII. Ecclesden Manor is a long, low Tudor-style house built in 1634. We are at the hub of the village, with the war memorial in the foreground. The Village Stores has a sign advertising Oxo on the shopfront. The scene is little different today.

ANGMERING

THE VILLAGE GREEN c1955 / A52004

An isolated village of flint and brick cottages, to the west of Chichester. In the village are Adsdean, a gabled Tudor style house of around 1850, and the parish church of St Mary, built in 1859. Northbrook Watermill is in very flat country nearby. The Stores is seen next door to a thatched house and restaurant. The shop is now a house, although Halliday's restaurant is still trading.

FUNTINGTON

THE VILLAGE c1960 / F160014

A fishing village and yachting centre located on a creek of Chichester Harbour. A straight and wide road leading to the quay creates an impression of past importance. The Romans, the Saxons and the Vikings used the area for invasion. In later centuries fishing was an important industry. The roadway can flood at very high tides. A two-masted sailing ship lies in a mud berth, a washing line post leans on the beach and women in long skirts stand and look towards the harbour.

BOSHAM

THE VILLAGE 1902 / 48336

This sizeable hamlet on the Downs south of Harting has no church, but boasts some attractive flint cottages and fine scenery. There is plenty of history here: Bow Hill was a great Stone Age centre on the Downs and there is the site of a Roman villa nearby. A local mansion, Watergate House, is now demolished. The signboard of the Victoria Inn is visible to the left of the picture. The scene today is little changed.

WEST MARDEN

THE VILLAGE C1955 / W614002

We are east of Bognor Regis. The poet William Blake lived in the village for four years. The medieval church of St Mary can be seen in the background of the picture. A four-wheeled cart is pulled by two horses in tandem and appears to be loaded with brushwood faggots; all of the action is halted whilst waiting patiently for the photographer. There is a fine flint garden wall in the foreground.

FELPHAM

THE VILLAGE 1903 / 50211

SIDLESHAM

THE QUAY c1960 / S589162

Sidlesham is a hamlet near Pagham Harbour. The 13th-century church of St Mary is built of stone rubble, not the usual flint of the area. Mapson's Farm was built in 1796. At high tides the sea comes very close to the fronts of the buildings. A range of cars waits on the roadway—let us hope they are above the high water line.

INDEX